THE KĀHUNA
Versatile Masters of Old Hawai'i

Legends and traditions of the ancient priesthood.

Coconut Shell Cups
for Ceremonial 'Awa Drinking
2½" high x 4" wide x 5¼" long

THE KĀHUNA

Versatile Masters
of Old Hawaiʻi

by
Likeke R. McBride

He ala ʻololī kō nā kāhuna.
Narrow is the path of the kāhuna.

Petroglyph Press

Dedicated to my friends
Walter and Marie Kuettel and Sparks, Susan and John Rodrigues
of Volcano, Hawai'i

Publisher's Note
In this edition, new photos and illustrations have been added and the text has been reset, revising the Hawaiian words to reflect currently accepted spelling and punctuation. Any suggestions, comments or corrections are welcomed. Enjoy!

Photo & Illustration Credits
Hawaiian Kapa and footed stone mortar with pounder on cover and artifacts on pages 2, 20 and 45 from the E.M. Tulman collection.

Photos of artifacts on cover and pages 2, 20 and 45 by Norman Makio, Modern Camera.

Line drawings on pages 12, 13, 15, 22, 26, 27, 34, 37, 41, 42, 43, 47, 49, 50, 52, 58 by L.R. McBride.

Etchings on pages 16, 36, 51, 52, 56, 66 by John Webber.

Line drawings on pages 21 & 40 by Eva Anderson.

Petroglyph photo on page 24 by A.S. McBride.

Photos on pages 29 & 39 by Rick Frederick.

Pele drawing on page 33 by Mark Waters.

Cover design and cover printing by Don O'Reilly, Hilo Bay Printing.

Published by the Petroglyph Press, Ltd.
160 Kamehameha Avenue • Hilo, Hawai'i 96720
Phone 808-935-6006 / Fax 808-935-1553
BBinfo@BasicallyBooks.com / www.BasicallyBooks.com

ISBN 0-912180-51-X

CONTENTS

Foreword 7

Who Were the Kāhuna? 9

The Origins of the Kāhuna 13

The Versatile Kāhuna 21

Astronomers and Navigators 22

Botanists and Agriculturists 26

The Geologists 29

The Meteorologists 34

Artists and Poets 36

Healers 42

Other Professions 51

Sorcerers 53

The Power of Words 60

In Conclusion 64

Additions and Corrections 1983 65

Bibliography 68

Additions and Corrections 2000 69

Bibliography 2000 72

Glossary 73

About the Author 74

FOREWORD
by Andrew S. McBride

$\mathscr{I}$ am honored to have been able to assist David and Christine Reed of Petroglyph Press in a minor revision of *The Kāhuna*. Written by my father, Likeke R. McBride, *The Kāhuna* was first published in 1972; a revision with important additions and corrections was published in 1983.

Part of this book's enduring value is the knowledge imparted and the respect with which it is provided. Dad loved Hawai'i, the Hawaiian people, and was profoundly affected by the genius of Hawaiian civilization. One example of its genius is the brilliant achievement of nā kāhuna.

I am very proud of Dad's work including this book and of the fact that he helped stimulate interest in Hawaiian culture and traditions in a career spanning over 30 years as scholar and author, entertainer, educator, and craftsman.

His approach in writing this book was significant. He understood and presented the kāhuna in a Hawaiian context, in my opinion its only legitimate context. Dad clarified our knowledge of the kāhuna, and downplayed the longstanding, widespread perception that kāhuna were merely "witch doctors" or sorcerers.

The use of "Big Kahuna" in certain television shows, movies, and in commercial snacks is misuse and cultural appropriation which does nothing to help us understand nā kāhuna of old Hawai'i.

As appealing as the kāhuna might be to people interested in New Age matters, it strikes me as a misreading of the kāhuna and as cultural appropriation also. This even though the appropriation might be sympathetic to the achievements of the Hawaiians.

Today the prestige of being linked to kāhuna is undeniable. Hawaiians - some very prominent - state their descent from kāhuna lines proudly and without reservation. It was not always this way; for 150 years nā kāhuna were suppressed. Recently, a local resident of O'ahu confided in me that she was studying to become a kahuna right after she explained her interests in the power of crystals and other New Age concerns.

Interest in nā kāhuna continues to grow. Kahuna traditions continue to affect culture, life and events in Hawai'i and the world. In late May 1998, a writer for the *Honolulu Advertiser* reported that Iwi'ula Aupuni, a Hawaiian kahuna living in Seattle, Washington, blessed USS Missouri - the famous beloved battleship - for its voyage to Pearl Harbor, Hawai'i under tow. A large photograph of Iwi'ula Aupuni blessing the battleship was featured in a prominent front page article.

When the kā'ai (sennit caskets) believed to contain the sacred bones of Līloa and Lonoikamakahiki were discovered missing from Bernice Pauahi Bishop Museum in Honolulu in early 1994, prominent Hawaiians discussed the disposition of the kā'ai. Kumu hula Frank K. Hewett wrote a letter to the *Advertiser* editor that the "kahuna tradition should decide the disposition of the kā'ai." In another letter to the editor published that day distinguished scholar Rubellite K. Johnson argued differently and concluded with a statement that "reviving the kahu (priestly) office for this particular kā'ai ... has grave implications."

Our store of knowledge about the kāhuna continues to grow with the publication of new books. Malcolm Nāea Chun translated and edited the *1867 Report of the 'Ahahui Lā'au Lapa'au of Wailuku, Maui on Native Hawaiian Health*. Chun's translation and careful examination of this text has given us additional information about the medical kahuna, names of practitioners and their teachers and knowledge of medical practices - particularly of Maui in the first half of the 1800's. This newly translated text recovered much information perhaps thought lost forever. This book also discounts any lingering belief that the Hawaiians acted passively in the face of devastating foreign diseases.

Chun's examination and translation of other Hawaiian language texts has added to what is known of the kāhuna and Hawaiian medical practices. His biographies of Davida Malo, S. N. Hale'ole and S. M. Kamakau, gathered in *Nā Kukui Pio 'Ole: The Inextinguishable Torches*, provide additional information about these scholars as important sources for information concerning the kāhuna. In particular, Hale'ole wrote about the Hawaiian Priesthood.

In conclusion, interest in the kāhuna continues to grow. The tradition, while greatly diminished due to terrible losses in the Hawaiian population from diseases introduced since contact with foregners, is regaining some of its strength and acceptance. This is a promising development.

Perhaps it is time to gather all of what we do know about the kāhuna, and subject the knowledge and its sources to careful examination and deep synthesis. Thus, we can attempt to piece together more of our fragmentary knowledge of the kāhuna, speculate carefully and learn even more. In time our understanding may yet deepen.

In *'Olelo No'eau: Hawaiian Proverbs and Poetical Sayings*, Mary Kawena Pukui wrote:

Ua lehulehu a manomano ka 'ikeha a ka Hawai'i
(Great and without end is the knowledge of the Hawaiians)

As we learn more about the kāhuna and their abilities and knowledge, this beautiful phrase continues to ring true.

Me ka pono,
Andrew S. McBride
Mililani, Hawai'i

WHO WERE THE KĀHUNA?

*I*n ancient Hawai'i, kāhuna were far more than the priests of a religious order. They were the doctors, architects, scientists, educators and agriculturists of their time. On them devolved the responsibility of conserving the resources, advancing knowledge, and meeting new situations within the framework of natural laws and human nature. They were the educated professionals of their time.

The kāhuna were persons of real ability. They arrived at their position only after more than two decades of training in a strict discipline. Steadying and upholding their judgment were the observations of untold generations of their predecessors.

The members of a kāhuna order were largely drawn from the ranks of the ruling class (ali'i), selected as children on the basis of intelligence, interest, and willingness to learn. Occasionally a child of exceptional ability might be accepted from the common people, but it was seldom difficult to trace his blood line to a royal family. Although girls were admitted to some orders, they were banned from some places and ceremonies and confined during menstruation.

The classes (papa) of kāhuna were divided into many orders. Although each was a specific school, the various introductory aspects ('ike kumu) often overlapped, supplanting a general course of instruction for all. Students were required to watch, listen and learn. Questions were discouraged, if not forbidden, and the scholars ('imi 'ike) were encouraged to think, to perceive and to ponder.

The location of some schools for priests is known, such as Halehale-ka-lani which was associated with Hikiau heiau at Nāpo'opo'o, Hawai'i, but there is scant information on the teaching methods and even less on the curriculum (a'o). We can surmise from other places in Polynesia that instruction began at dawn and continued as long as the sun was ascending. As a small child, the student learned the laws of the gods (kānāwai), the lesser regulations (kaka'ina), and the restrictions (kāpu) of the school. He was taught to observe, to seek and to experiment within certain limits. In time, he became a master of psychology and used his knowledge of human nature to make predictions, accomplish desired ends and strengthen the order to which he belonged. He learned to employ skills like hypnosis, auto-suggestion, mimicry, and ventriloquism which are even today held in awe by a majority of people even though these skills have been stripped of their

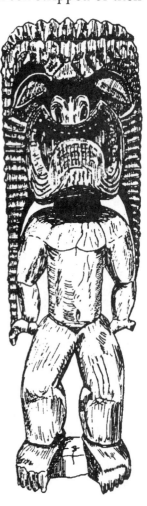

mystique. He was taught that these aptitudes were direct manifestations of the gods, granted to a certain few.

Schools differed as did instructors, for not all were equal in ability to either demonstrate or teach. When kāhuna of the same order from different places met, the common query was, "Who taught you?" (Na wai 'oe i a'o). A kahuna never forgot his instructor and always mentioned him in his prayers.

Each priestly order had its own god. A kahuna believed in the gods and in the power of prayer. If a branch of learning was being taught by someone indifferent to the god of that instruction (laukana) then the knowledge of that branch could not be passed on by that person. A kahuna had to have faith in his gods and in his ability to communicate with them. Much of his training consisted of faultlessly memorizing long chants and rituals. He was taught that his accomplishments were the result of gaining the favor of the gods by successfully performing perfect ritual.

The ancient prayer of the kāhuna from the temple tower was "Let that which is unknown become known." It was hoped that during his apprenticeship each priest would learn fast ('a'apo), obtain great patience (ahaloa) and strive to obtain understanding (na'i), that he might become a lover of wisdom and knowledge (akeakamai) and be able to peer into the depths of his profession as the fisherman can look into the sea when he has put kukui oil on the water.

At the graduation ceremony ('ailolo), the students themselves agreed upon the member of the class who had surpassed all of the rest in learning, and that student was then given the choice part of the commencement pig in the final ritual, an honor much like that of valedictorian today.

No matter how able the student became in a particular field of endeavor, he was not as advanced as a person who had become proficient in two professional skills. Even if he excelled (hiapa'i'ole) beyond all others in one field, he was not considered a high priest. Only a kahuna who had become adept in many fields could be called a high priest, and only one who had mastered all learning was given the highest title puhi okaoka. Becoming a consummate priest was particularly difficult because the Hawaiian tutor seldom imparted all of his wisdom before taking to his deathbed lest one of his students surpass him. A favored scholar was generally called just before the teacher's dying to wipe the lips of the master (hikianakopili) and gain the final knowledge.

The accomplishments of these versatile masters of old Hawai'i were formidable, and yet, despite their keen observation and great dedication, they sometimes were baffled or arrived at conclusions that were in error. The land breeze that rarely wafts the chill air of Mauna Loa down across the broad expanse of Puna was considered beyond comprehension (kapolakā). The old poetry ponders "the beautiful sweet mystery of the gentle, cooling Pu'ulena wind." Boils appearing on the body resulted, the kāhuna believed, from the sorcerer's evil. Moles were construed to be indications of the character of the one they were on, although some kāhuna thought they were the result of flies.

The origin of lava trees was a problem that confounded modern geologists a little over a generation ago. In an old chant, a kahuna hypothesizes that they were petrified by the strong sulfurous fumes of eruptive activity, although people commonly believed that they were persons who had met Pele's wrath. Clouds were a puzzle of sorts as well. They could be used to forecast events and therefore were undoubtedly the work of the gods. The kāhuna reasoned that the clouds brought rain (children were told rain was spillage from an astral lake) but thought that the clouds were created by fire.

We are just now beginning to appreciate the strides that the Hawaiian kāhuna had made in many endeavors, and to investigate the things that may prove of value to our society. Some who read this book may, in the years to come, owe their lives to the knowledge accrued by the priests of old Hawai'i. There is little doubt among some medical men today that the doctors of pre-historic Hawai'i were able to arrest cancer, heart trouble, and other illnesses. Similar discoveries in the fields of agriculture, fishing, and conservation may prove to be of great future benefit. The accomplishments of the kāhuna are difficult to reconstruct and appraise today because so much has been lost or concealed. What little we know and comprehend will nevertheless stand as a monument to the innate intelligence of mankind.

Lava Trees

THE ORIGINS OF THE KĀHUNA

$\mathscr{T}$he history of the priesthood (mo'o kahuna) proceeds from a simple structure in antiquity toward a constantly more complex one. Back in the traditional homeland in the beginning of time, the specialist in prayer and worship was the first to be recognized. According to S.M. Kamakau in *Ka Po'e Kahiko*, "The separation began with the priesthood order of Līhau'ula, the first child of Kahikoluamea and older brother of Wakea. This order, the papa kahuna pule, was the first to be selected out (wae) and so kahuna orders were kept separate throughout the entire race in the following generations."

At a much later date perhaps, the medical aspect of the priesthood was set apart. This was probably influenced by the increased importance of the physician to the population, although the arrival of foreigners like the 'Alaneo, said to have been hermaphrodite healers from Kahiki, may have had something to do with it.

On two or three occasions in the legendary past, strange epidemics threatened to annihilate the people, leaving only a few survivors to repopulate the land. Perhaps because of the depredations by illness and disease the Hawaiians venerated the men of medicine.

Some of the early medical men like Koleamoku, who first learned to use herbs in healing, were apotheosized. Another who was elevated to such a state was Lonopūhā. S.M.

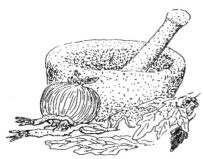

Kamakau relates, "The kahuna hāhā belonged to the order of Lono - that is Lonopūhā. It was a very ancient order of medical kāhuna. The work of these kāhuna was to feel for the disease, to locate it, and to prescribe for it. The original kahuna (po'o kahuna mua) of this order was Kamakanui'āha'ilono. He showed his skill and knowledge in the treatment of Lono, a chief of Ka'ū, Hawai'i...." Lonopūhā became a follower of the master Kamakanui'āha'ilono, at length assumed the head of the medical profession and eventually was deified.

Palaha, the discoverer of the benefits of the enema, did his initial research on a dog and also did an autopsy to determine the nature of his father's fatal malady. For these things he and his father were placed in the succession of Lonopūhā kāhuna.

There is scarcely a people of note from the earliest times that have not had prophets of one sort or another. The people of Hawai'i were no exception. These were for the most part a class (papa) of kāhuna called kāula but occasionally someone outside the order was inexplicably inspired (ulu kau).

Lūhaukapawa is said to have been the first prophet recognized and the last was Kapihe, in the time of King Kamehameha, who foresaw that, "The islands will be united, the kapu of the gods overthrown, those of the heavens (the chiefs) will be brought low, and those of the earth (the common people) will be raised up."

One of the oft quoted prophecies still held valid today is that of Kaopulupulu at the drowning of his son by the minions of his brother. As the boy struggled against being pushed into the ocean, his father called, "It is better in the sea, for from the sea shall come the life of the land."

There are interesting similarities in certain aspects of the priesthood with those in other countries. In Hawai'i, the first victim on the battlefield was scalped and the trophy (elehua) was offered to the god of war. Almost the same ritual was conducted in millennium earlier by the Asians who founded Japan on the islands wrested from the Caucasian *Ainu*. There are also remarkable resemblances to Hawaiian priestly customs found in the chronicles of the conquerors of Mexico, as well as those in other places around the Pacific.

When the ancient seafarers of Hawai'i sailed to lands beyond the sky, they returned with new plants, new ideas and, most important, brought back men of knowledge — new

blood for the priesthood. Some of these are described as being light skinned and having eyes that differed from those of the Hawaiians. The following tale of the men brought back by Paumakua is taken from *Account of the Polynesian Race* by Abraham Fornander.

"One of the legends relates that of Paumakua, on his return from one of his foreign voyages, brought back with him to O'ahu two white men said to have been priests A-ua-ka-hinu and A-ua-ka-mea, afterwards named Kae-Kae and Maliu, from whom several priestly families in after ages claimed descent and authority." These persons were described as:

"Ka haole nui maka 'ālohilohi
(*A large foreigner, bright sparkling eyes*)
A āholehole maka 'a'ā
(*White cheeks, roguish staring eyes*)
Ka pua'a ke'oke'o nui maka 'ula'ula!
(*A great white pig with reddish eyes!*)

"In later years of Hawaiian history, two of the most prominent high priests in all the islands were among the descendants of these foreigners."

The structure of Hawaiian religion was altered considerably during the twelfth century. Traditionally, credit for the changes is given to Pā'ao, a strange white priest who came to Hawai'i from Upolu, Samoa, where he had lands.

Pā'ao might have spent all of his life in Samoa had it not been for family troubles. His brother accused Pā'ao's eldest son of stealing fruit from his trees. The boy hotly denied the charge and demanded that his father open his stomach to prove beyond a doubt that the crime was not his. His uncle

Heiau at Waimea, Kaua'i. Illustration by John Webber.

agreed that this indeed was the only way to discover the truth and insisted that Pāʻao would find within the boy undigested remains of the fruit the son had stolen.

The operation performed by Pāʻao substantiated the boy's innocence but took his life. In bitterness, Pāʻao decided to leave that land of sorrow and had his great vessel made ready for a voyage. The day before sailing, the son of Pāʻao's brother happened to come by to watch the activity and, in a final act of revenge for losing his own son, Pāʻao had the boy killed and buried in the sand beneath his vessel, so that the body would not be discovered until his departure. No sooner had he left the shore than a number of priests called to Pāʻao from the cliff and asked him to return for them. He told them that was not possible but that he would take any who could fly to the ship. Accordingly, several were dashed to death on the rocks below during the attempt. A few got to the vessel, while the rest stayed to face the wrath of Pāʻao's brother.

When Pāʻao arrived in Hawaiʻi, he reputedly brought with him the concept of making images. On the southern shore of Hawaiʻi, in the district of Puna, he built a temple far different from the simple religious platforms familiar to the island people. The heiau or temple was not a single flat structure but a complex of platforms with thatched buildings on them and three-storied towers covered with white kapa cloth, all surrounded by a long stone wall. At the entrance to the temple stood a huge wooden cross (peʻa).

Because of the cross and the information that some of the earliest images had, the head on the chest below the shoulder line with the arms upraised like a crude crucifix, some scholars have entertained the notion that the strange white priest Pāʻao was a Catholic friar. (Just a few miles from the spot where Pāʻao built his temple, in the village of Kalapana in Puna, is a Catholic church named Star of the Sea. In that tiny church, the most remarkable painting is the first "station of the cross" which pictures a black robed figure with the name Pāʻao printed below.)

The new temple soon became well known, for the priests scoured the island to find all manner of medicinal plants and herbs to transplant within its walls. According to tradition, it became a sort of medical college where the graduates were permitted to wear the red robe of the physician. Because of this, the temple was called 'Aha'ula, red robe or sacred assembly.

The second temple of Pā'ao, Mo'okini heiau, was constructed on the northern tip of the island of Hawai'i, which was renamed Upolu after the place in Samoa that the white priest had come from. The missionary Reverend William Ellis visited that spot during his famous walk around the island in 1823. In his journal, he wrote "... we resumed our journey, and proceeded towards the north point of the island, near which we passed through the district of Pauepu, in which formerly stood a temple called Mokini, celebrated in the historical accounts of the Hawaiians, as built by Pā'ao, a foreign priest, who resided in Pauepu, and officiated in this temple."

"A tradition preserved among them states that in the reign of Kahoukapu, a kahuna (priest) arrived at Hawai'i from a foreign country; that he was a white man, and brought with him two idols or gods, one large, and the other small; that they were adopted by the people, and placed among the Hawaiian gods; that the above mentioned temple of Mokini was erected for them, where they were worshipped according to

Unusual Ancient Wood Image in Bishop Museum

the direction of Pā'ao, who became a powerful man in the nation. The principal event preserved of his life, however, respects a child of Kahoukapu, whose mother was a woman of humble rank, but which was spared at the solicitations of Pā'ao. After his death, his son Opiri officiated in his temple; and the only particular worthy of note in their account of his life, is his acting as interpreter between the king and a party of white men who arrived at the island."

Reverend Ellis continues: "... (They) landed somewhere in the south-west part of the island, and repaired to the mountains, where they took up their abode. The native regarded them with a superstitious curiosity and dread, and knew not whether to consider them as gods or men.

"Opiri was sent for by the king of that part of the island where they were residing, and consulted as to the conduct to be observed towards them.

"According to his advice, a large present of provisions was cooked and carried to them. Opiri led the procession, accompanied by several men, each carrying a bamboo cane, with a piece of white native cloth tied to the end of it.

"When the strangers saw them approaching their retreat, they came out to meet them. The natives placed the baked pigs and potatoes, etc. on the grass, fixed their white banners in the ground and then retreated a few paces. The foreigners approached. Opiri addressed them. They answered, received the presents, and afterwards conversed with the people through the medium of Opiri. The facility with which they could communicate their thoughts by means of Opiri, the governor said, was attributed to the supposed influence of Opiri with his gods.

"The foreigners they imagined were supernatural beings, and as such were treated with every possible mark of respect. After remaining some time on the island, they returned to their own country."

Sometime during the five or six hundred years of operation, the temples of Pā'ao became luakini, places of human sacrifice. The temple of 'Aha'ula gained such a reputation that it was shunned by the people and became known as Waha'ula, figuratively, bloody mouth.

It has been advanced that if the first temple of Pā'ao was in reality a kind of medical school, then the human sacrifice practiced at Waha'ula may have begun as a result of vivisection for teaching students or operations conducted either as investigation or healing attempts. These were in time corrupted to a ritual of death to propitiate some of the gods.

Pā'ao won the goodwill of the common people by engineering a successful rebellion against the harsh King Kama'iole. After the tyrant was put to death, the people gladly would have made Pā'ao king in his stead, but the priest refused the crown saying that his was the work of the gods. With the agreement of the council of chiefs, he sent to Upolu, Samoa for the chief Pili who was made sovereign and began a line of kings that extended to the time of Kamehameha. At the same time, a line of priests begotten by Pā'ao endured an equal period, and one, Hewahewa, ended what the white priest had begun by destroying the temples when the kapu system and the priesthood fell in 1819.

Stone Pounder (3" high x 1½" wide),
Stone Kahuna Bowl (2¼" high x 3¼" wide),
Coconut Shell 'Awa Cup (2½" high x 4" wide x 5¼" long)

THE VERSATILE KĀHUNA

*E*ach of the Hawaiian Islands in ancient times appeared to have one or more centers of culture and achievement. Often these corresponded to the residence areas of the highest chief, but on some of the islands they may have been more permanent than on others.

It seems likely that the seat of science on the island of Hawai'i was in the district of Puna, the beginning of the land. Here, on the easternmost point of the Big Island, was an astronomical observatory of sorts, a school of navigation, a meteorological station and a college of medicine. Here too, Pele, the volcano goddess, put on some of her most beautiful and awesome displays, which have been observed and speculated upon for more than a thousand years.

Unfortunately, most of the early visitors who queried the Hawaiians about their progress in some of the sciences knew much less about the subject than the natives they questioned. Others evinced strong tendencies to discredit Hawaiian knowledge even before sampling it, and lumped it all as heathen superstition. In examining the accomplishments of the Hawaiians then, it must be borne in mind that we have only fragments of their scientific knowledge. Much of what they knew and could do died with the last of the masters.

ASTRONOMERS AND NAVIGATORS

Innumerable are the stars
The large stars
The small stars
The red stars of Kāne, O infinite space
The great moon of Kāne
The great sun of Kāne
Moving, floating
Set moving about in the great space of Kāne
The great earth of Kāne
The rain encircled earth of Kāne
The earth that Kāne set in motion
Moving are the stars, moving is the moon
Moving is the great earth of Kāne.

Ancient chant

𝒪f the innumerable stars seen from the islands, only a few can be called by Hawaiian names today. Unfortunately, the early European visitors who were competent to record the names correctly were primarily interested in those stars which they used for navigation and seem to have neglected those exceeding third magnitude. Thus, of the several thousand stars which may be seen from Hawai'i, only the names of about 120 have been retained.

Only a few of the star groups of the Hawaiians correspond with the Euphratean constellations familiar to people of western culture. The Big Dipper was called Nā-hiku (The Seven), Gemini was known as Ka-māhana (The Twins), and the Hawaiians recognized the Pleiades as Makali'i (Little Eyes).

The Hawaiian constellations more nearly fit the smaller groups astronomers called asterisms. For example, the Hyades cluster in the head of Taurus was named Ka-nuku-o-ka-puahi, the belt and sword of Orion was called Nā-kao, the line of three stars in Aquila was known as Humu-mā and probably Lyra plus the star Vega was Keoe. We have the names of more than twenty-five, and there must have been many times that number identified by the kāhuna. Other things in the night sky were named as well. The Milky Way was Kau and its detached portions, the Magellanic Clouds, were Pulelehua Kea for the larger and Pulelehua Uli for the smaller.

Despite the differences in nomenclature, astronomy in Hawai'i (sans mathematics) was at about the same stage as in Europe in the early seventeenth century, prior to the adoption of the telescope. An earlier invention, which set European astronomers apart from the Hawaiians, was the timepeace which enabled them to calculate the equinox in order to adjust their calendar.

The Hawaiian astronomer (kilo hōkū) arrived at a similar solution of regulating the lunar calendar by using the means at hand. It was known that the ecliptic (heleakalā) changes slowly throughout the year and, because of this, the sun rises at a different point on the horizon, shuttling between the two extremes. Once the northernmost and southernmost points (solstices) were fixed, the equinox could be measured halfway between them. This was done at the observatory on the eastern point of Hawai'i at the place called Ha'eha'e, where the great stones caught the sun. By such means, the astronomers could determine the nineteen year cycle of 235 lunar months by which solar and lunar years are harmonized, and in so doing learn to utilize the cycle of 223 lunar months enabling them to predict eclipses.

It is not surprising that there was no separation between astronomy and astrology. The predictability of events in the firmament naturally led the Hawaiians to seek correlations with earthly things. From long experience, the kāhuna had learned that the phases of the moon influenced crops, weather, fishing and the behavior of men. The other travelers of the night, such a planets (hōkū lewa or hōkū 'ae'a), meteors (koli or akua lele), and comets (hōkū welowelo) were thought to have a special importance in determining future events.

Pu'uloa petroglyph which may depict voyaging.

Perhaps the most skilled of all the professional astronomers were the navigators. These were not just coastal pilots
but were men capable of crossing more than two thousand
miles of ocean and returning home without the aid of a compass, sextant or chronometer. To do this they had to memo-
rize a fantastic amount of specific information. It was known
that the stars and planets appear to move in circular paths
(ala po'ai) around a fixed star (hōkū-pa'a) which we call Po-
laris or the North Star.

Each star that rises from or sinks below a specific place
on the horizon (lua), is an unfailing indication of a point of
the compass. Since a star could only be used as a guide (ihukū)
as long as it was near the horizon, the navigator had to know
the other stars in the same circle. These were taught in schools
of navigation like the one near the eastern point of Hawai'i.

By the time the potential navigator finished the many
years of study required, he had become virtually a human
computer capable of recalling with clarity the rising and set-
ting points of over 120 stars as they changed throughout the
year. The students were also taught the directions of certain
foreign lands from alignments of stones and, in addition, the
seas, the winds and the weather found along the way.

Many of the storied voyages to distant lands cannot be assigned to a particular period of time. It may have been a thousand years ago that the great seafarer Olopana came back from a foreign land with a tall barbarian who wore the hides of animals to cover his fair skin. As a result, perhaps, few names have become so popular in Hawaiian tradition.

During the twelfth and thirteenth centuries, several voyages were made to the southern islands. In the chant of Kaulu, it is said that he visited Vavau, Upolu, Kahiki (Tahiti) and other lands. A generation later, the kahuna Kamahualele navigated the vessels of Mōʻīkeha to Borabora and back, only to repeat the entire trip years later with the old chief's son. About the same period, the navigator Paumakua sailed to a far place and returned with several priests with light skin (haole), large size and bright shining eyes.

In the following centuries, either no adventurers set out for distant lands or, perhaps more likely, none returned. Kahiki ceased to be thought of as a particular place and became instead a general word meaning simply abroad. Sometime in the sixteenth or seventeenth century, Kūaliʻi, the last great voyager, found a different Kahiki.

Kahiki, land where Olopana dwelt
The land is within and the sun is without
And the land is indistinct.
Perhaps you have seen it — I have seen it
I have truly seen Kahiki,
Kahiki where the language is strange.
To Kahiki belong the people who
Ascend the backbone of heaven
And gaze down upon us.
There are none like us in Kahiki
Kahiki has only the haole
They are like gods
I am like a man, wandering about
And the only one that ever got there!
                              from the chant of Kūaliʻi

BOTANISTS AND AGRICULTURISTS

$\mathcal{L}$ong before Linnaeus devised plant taxonomy, the kāhuna in Hawai'i had already evolved a classification system which consisted of groups and sub-groups used to identify certain plants. A general name was given to associate those plants having certain characteristics such as a'e, pilo, hāpu'ū, koki'o, and 'ōhi'a to name a few. The plant was then given an additional name to type the bloom or some other trait and, sometimes, another word was added to identify still further some particular characteristic.

For example, using 'ōhi'a as the general name, lehua was added to describe the feathery nature of the bloom. In addition, the color of the blossom is described or another trait is included to name the tree exactly.

'Ōhi'a lehua 'āpane	*Red bloomed* 'ōhi'a
'Ōhi'a lehua pōlena	*Yellow blossomed* 'ōhi'a
'Ōhi'a lehua puakea	*White blossomed* 'ōhi'a
'Ōhi'a lehua 'ai	'Ōhi'a *with edible fruit*
'Ōhi'a hā	'Ōhi'a *with tiny edible fruit*
'Ōhi'a maka noe	*A Kaua'i shrub*
'Ōhi'a lehua haole	*Foreign* 'ōhi'a

1 inch

'Ōhi'a lehua

The names of plants were not consistent throughout the islands, however, and sometimes even varied from one district to another. In addition, many of the herbs used in medicine were known to the kāhuna by special names, perhaps to keep their use a trade secret. In some instances, a garden of medicinal plants was a part of a heiau and in it, under carefully controlled conditions, plants from all over an island were grown.

The Hawaiians were diligent farmers with a love of growing things, who followed age old traditions by planting in season during certain phases of the moon and with elaborate ceremony. This is a workable system which has been used in Europe and Asia for thousands of years and still is employed in parts of America today. Plants were believed to respond to affection and care, and the farmer often encouraged or scolded his leafy wards so that they might do their best.

The agricultural expert (kahuna ho'oulu'ai) advised when a crop should be rotated, when a field should remain fallow and when the land was ahulu and should be sweetened with the addition of rotted hau leaves. When new land was cleared, the brush was burned on the field and the ashes scattered. In cultivating, the weeds were left to decompose so that their strength might be added to the soil.

Little is known of the horticultural tricks of the experts in old Hawai'i, but we do know some of the results. By the time of Captain Cook's arrival in the islands in 1779, they had developed several sorts of yams, 24 kinds of sweet potatoes, 70 types of bananas and 350 varieties of taro or kalo. The latter was probably the most important crop. The botanist Dr. Otto Degener estimates that since the entire plant is eaten, one square mile of intensively cultivated taro would feed 15,000 people indefinitely.

Where valleys permitted, wet land taro was cultivated in bottoms by planting the crop in small hills (kipa) and using the adjacent stream for irrigation. Where the land sloped, terraces (lo'i) of wet land taro were watered by an extensive system of sluices to convey the precious fluid to the places where it was needed.

Taro or Kalo

In the uplands, and more arid areas, dry land taro and
sweet potatoes were the staple crops. When the plants were
young, the rows were covered with fern fronds to help con-
serve moisture and later weeds were pulled and banked
against the plants for the same purpose. Traces of some of
the old upland farms can still be seen today in aerial surveys.
On the mountainsides, the fields were laid out in plots con-
forming to the contour of the land, bordered by sugar cane
and bananas.

John Sutter of California was so impressed with the agricultural ability of the Hawaiians that he persuaded several
of the experts and farmers to return with him to the Sacra-
mento River country in 1839. It was there, nearly a decade
later, that their work was destroyed by the gold rush. Even
so, it was food imported from Hawai'i that helped feed the
multitude seeking riches until the madness died away.

Hawaiian man pounding poi from taro or kalo roots.

THE GEOLOGISTS

"$\mathscr{G}$eology is a combination of observation and uncommon sense," Dr. Robert Bates of Ohio State University once declared. The natural blending of these traits in the kāhuna made them well acquainted with the volcanic land they inhabited. There existed experts who specialized in earth study (kilohonua) and those who knew the configuration of the landscape (huli honua), as well as those of other disciplines who used geologic methods in their work, such as the agricultural expert and the architect. Surveyors especially had to know the features of the landscape (hi'ohi'ona). The kahu who sought suitable secret caves for burial probably employed the principles of practical volcanic geology.

The specialists of olden times that most nearly fit what we think of as geologists could do some things that few "rock doctors" of these times could emulate. It is claimed that an expert of the highest order could be shown a rock specimen from any district on the island of Hawai'i and he could name the kind of rock and the place it cropped out (hū honua).

Rocks were classified as to density, use and color. Because different islands sometimes had different names for similar specimens and since often there were local names as well, there is some confusion as to the number of differentiated rocks for which we still have names. In all likelihood, each of three categories contained over two dozen types that could be readily identified by the expert.

'A'ā and Pāhoehoe Lava Flows

Bird's-eye view of Kīlauea Caldera

Modern geologists the world over have adopted the Hawaiian terms 'a'ā and pāhoehoe to distinguish between rough and smooth lava flows. Perhaps someday they will accept others such as kīpuka for untouched land encircled by lava and lauoho-o-Pele (Pele's hair) for the natural fiber glass produced by fountains of melted rock.

The stories of Pele, the volcano goddess, tell much of what the professionals of old knew about the geology of Hawai'i. The legends relate that Pele landed first at unnamed islands far to the northwest and then came to Kaua'i and proceeded down the island chain searching for an ideal home site.

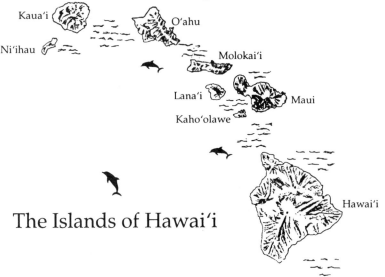

Kaua'i

Ni'ihau

O'ahu

Molokai'i

Lana'i

Maui

Kaho'olawe

Hawai'i

The Islands of Hawai'i

At the places she stopped, she tested the ground but none was found suitable. At last she came to the island of Hawai'i, landed at the place of quiet burning and at length climbed to the top of Kīlauea where she found the perfect conditions she sought for her abode.

The legendary stops of Pele along the Hawaiian island chain correspond exactly with the order in which geologists today believe the islands were created. The last stop where Pele finally made her home is not only the most active volcano in the islands but in the world as well.

The old stories also explain that after Pele drove away her newly wedded husband, Kamapua'a, they divided the land between them. All of the territory beyond Mauna Loa on Hawai'i and on the other islands was to belong to Kamapua'a, and all below that line was to be the land of Pele. This, too, corresponds with the thinking of modern geologists. The "land of Pele" contains the active volcanoes, while the volcanoes comprising the remainder of the high islands are thought to be dormant.

The legends of the volcano goddess disclose that a great deal was known about how the volcanoes worked. An old chant says:

> She comes first to the top of the mountain
> Young and beautiful, dancing in all her glory
> Then she sleeps, becomes old and ugly
> Moves through the hidden ways of the mountain
> To come out near the seashore
> Angry and capable of great destruction.

This cyclic type of volcano behavior has been observed often by geologists. The melted rock rises from thirty-five miles below to fill an enormous reservoir beneath the volcano summit. When there is pressure enough, the top of the mountain splits and melted rock spurts hundreds of feet into the air in beautiful fiery fountains. Following the summit eruption, the volcano is quiet and the top of the reservoir seems to seal itself off. Then, as the pressure increases from new melt coming up from depth, the magma begins to flow through the cracks and lava tubes which make up a rift zone, moving underground tens of miles down the mountain, to break out wherever the system is weakest.

One of the remarkable predictions is that given to Kamapua'a by Pele:

> Someday I will build for you a new island
> Another land in Hawai'i
> And there we will live together
> Forever in harmony

It is undoubtedly a coincidence that twenty-five miles south of Kīlauea lies another volcano, named Lō'ihi. Though entirely submerged, it is tremendous in size, with its top at least fifteen thousand feet above the ocean floor. Although it has erupted recently, geologists doubt that the event could be seen because the summit is still two thousand feet below sea level.

The Hawaiians are perhaps the only people who connected the occurrence of earthquakes, volcano eruptions and tidal waves. One wonders how they learned that the tsunami or tidal wave originated in distant lands and traveled across the ocean to strike Hawai'i. An old chant, however, is quite specific:

> *In far Kahiki*
> *Pele stamps the long wave*
> *The high wave*
> *The broad wave*
> *The wave that dashes the shores*
> *Of Hāmākua*
> *And of Hilo*
> *And overturns the land.*

To Pele is also attributed the lightning and it is not hard to understand their reasoning. When a phreatic or steam explosion occurs on the volcano, a tremendous cloud of rock dust and steam boils up thousands of feet into the air. Inside this turbulent cloud may be a lightning storm that can be seen for a great distance.

THE METEOROLOGISTS

It is quite possible that the longest used weather station in the world is near the eastern tip of the Big Island of Hawai'i. For over seven hundred years, a hill named Halekamahina, house of the moon, was the residence of the kāhuna called nānā uli, weather forecasters, and a school for those selected to learn the science of prediction. Very likely the kāhuna called kilo makani who observed the winds for the purpose of navigation and the nānā ao who used clouds for divining also worked there. "Thin is the weather forecaster from living on hills" is an old saying that might more aptly have been applied to the heiē, the apprentices whose job it was to carry the words of the weather prophet to those who used the information.

It is occasionally said that the Hawaiians needed no words to describe the weather, implying that the days are seldom less than perfect. While it is a difficult point to argue, the people of old apparently thought otherwise. Each change of the wind had a name which denoted its direction, strength and relative temperature. Every kind of rain was also named, taking into account its direction, duration and relative amount of falling precipitation. In short, the kāhuna had the means to describe any and all meteorological phenomena.

Spiral Petroglyph

These professional weathermen knew that during large storms the winds altered direction in a predictable fashion. They understood the portent of high cirrus clouds (lani hulu) and a mackerel sky (kaha'ea) and the behavior of birds and animals prior to certain kinds of weather. On a night during a long inclement period, if the stars didn't twinkle, the kāhuna would know that the weather was about to change and, in a day or so, good weather would return. Likewise a red sunset or the tops of towering cumulus clouds leaning a contrary direction to the wind indicated a weather change.

Some kāhuna relied upon observation of the action of natural or artificial whirlpools to forecast approaching storms. They believed that the water turned in one direction with the advent of "dirty" weather and circled the opposite way when the weather was going to be fair.

It seems correct to say that based on decades of study and untold generations of experience by his predecessors, the weather forecaster of old Hawai'i was probably as accurate in his predictions as the weather prophet of twenty years ago.

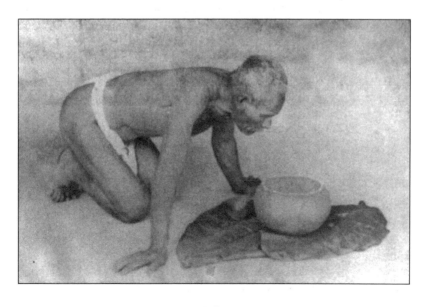

A Kahuna

ARTISTS AND POETS

*A*n entire book could be devoted to the role of the kāhuna in Hawaiian art. There was no area that the creative imagination (makakū) did not touch upon. The making of musical instruments, the hula, gourd decoration, utensil manufacture, ivory carving and jewelry making (kūpe'e) are only a few of the fields of art that were taught and practiced.

That Hawai'i excelled in many of the arts is due mainly to the training given to the master kāhuna in several fields. More elaborate sculpture and wood carving are found elsewhere in Polynesia, as is architecture, tattooing, shell work, ship design and stone carving. In a few phases of art, however, the Hawaiian of old had no peer.

Although primitive people the world over used feathers for adornment, none of their efforts equaled the craftsmanship and beauty of Hawai'i's featherwork. Tiny feathers of red and yellow, hardly larger than a fingernail, were tied shingle fashion to a very fine mesh net (nae). They were used to cover combs, fans, helmets, wicker images, mummy cases and were made into robes of various designs and colors.

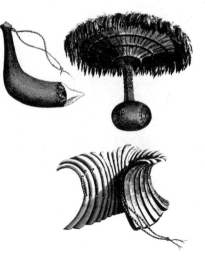

The kapa (tapa) of Hawai'i is outstanding for its quality and even more so for its many bright colors, in contrast to the black and brown motifs employed elsewhere in Polynesia. The most remarkable contrast of all is

Various Articles by John Webber

Kapa Stamps

that instead of being painted, most of the designs were printed. Captain Cook remarked that the designs were made so well that they rivaled the work of the mills of England.

The stamps with which the kapa was printed were made by carving experts. Bamboo strips and sometimes wooden blocks were the materials used. Designs that required a special skill and art were those which printed in one color while leaving an identical shape in the background color.

On the practical side, the Hawaiians also pioneered in the development of wet strength kapa that was able to withstand the rigors of swimming and surfing without going to pieces.

It is in the language arts that the kāhuna truly excelled. Whether a poet (haku mele), storyteller (kākā'ōlelo), or one who engaged in repartee (pāpā), he had to have an extensive knowledge of vocabulary and semantics. Being well versed in tradition, lore, mythology, and history (pa'a mo'olelo) and endowed with an excellent memory were essential.

While retention and recall were important in all of the endeavors of the kāhuna, these were indispensable in the language arts. If the priesthood had the ability to record symbols in a kind of writing, it may not have been developed enough to utilize for composition. Poetry, therefore, had to be conceived and constructed entirely in the mind of the poet, who had to forget the formulations which led to the final product while remembering the entire finished work.

Some poetry was composed by a committee of poets. One would suggest a line and the others would either reject it or polish and refine it until it was suitable for the final form. Line by line the free verse would be put together, revised, edited and, remarkably, remembered by all. Perhaps, at times, a person with an eidetic memory ('apo) might be employed. These people were so endowed that they could listen to hours of recitation and infallibly repeat it all days, months, or even years later. One of the missionaries tested such a person by reading the Bible to him for over an hour and at the end the old man recited for the same length of time all that had been read without a single error.

One of the beauties of Hawaiian compositions is that in each is something for everyone. Often a creation would embody as many as five different meanings. Each stanza might contain a literal meaning, a figurative meaning, a historical or a legendary reference, a sexual meaning and a hidden meaning (kaona). As a person grew in intelligence and understanding, he would be able to grasp more and more of the deeper meanings, eventually perhaps, to his great enjoyment, comprehending the entire work in depth. Look for the many different meanings in the following translation:

> Remember the days of our youth
> Swollen now are the clouds of Hanakahi
> Swelled now above the eyes is the cloud of morning
> In vain is the battle of children
> The great battle will follow
> As the deep sea follows shallow water
> The warrior arises
> Ready alike for victory or defeat.

Because of the vivid imagery, graceful rhythms and tremendous depth of meaning, Hawaiian poetry must be the finest in the world. It is unfortunate that so little has been preserved and that translations of what remains often fall far short of rendering the subtlety and multiple meanings that exist in the unrestrained, unrhymed verse of old Hawai'i.

The language art most frequently overlooked is that of

selecting names for places, things, and people. In olden times, the importance of names was fully recognized. In order to achieve the greatest power capable, a name was never just given, but carefully and painstakingly selected by a group of kāhuna who were semanticists or experts in the meanings of words.

The concept seems to be that in choosing a name, the more meanings that the name incorporated that were apt, the more power (mana) the appellation would contain. Such toponyms then legitimately used in name chants (mele 'inoa) and in other poetry would add their power to the whole.

For an example, the name of a black sand beach on the island of Hawai'i is Kaimū, a place famous (wahi pana) from remote times. A few of the meanings of Kaimū are these:

Kai mu — The silent sea

Kai Mū — The sea of the quiet, hirsute Menehune

Kai mu — The body catcher or strangler sea

Ka imu — The oven, after the way that unimportant visitors were figuratively roasted because the residents were used to VIP's.

Kai-mu — A contracted word meaning gathering (at the) sea (to watch surfing)

Kaimū Black Sand Beach, Kalapana, Hawai'i

Petroglyph Field

A few miles from Kaimū Black Sand Beach is a vast flat of
smooth lava covered with incised figures, designs and mark-
ings called petroglyphs. This particular spot called Pu'uloa
(figuratively, long life) is one of the larger fields in the state,
which possibly has more petroglyphs than any other place
on earth.

These rock carvings or ki'i pohaku are appreciated today
principally for their artistic merit, but less than a century and
a half ago they had a special significance to the people of
Hawai'i. During certain times, particular figures were daubed
with red ocher (kāpala ki'i) in ceremonies which are said to
be very old. This rite seems to have been shared by other
petroglyph areas in the world, notably those in eastern Sibe-
ria and in Sweden.

The missionary William Ellis dismissed the petroglyphs
of Hawai'i as "the first efforts of an uncivilized people toward the construction of a language of symbols." It is likely
that he either underestimated the ability of the Hawaiians or

was intentionally misled. Some of the old people have insisted that the kāhuna could "read" the petroglyphs and that they had a certain significance, but the majority of the people appear unaware that the drawings are more than doodling.

In many ancient cultures, the ability to read and write was confined entirely to the priesthood who used it as magic to strengthen their position. Recently deciphered is the picture script of the Inca priests which was not recognized as writing for 450 years.

Only one incident of a Hawaiian reading symbols has been recorded, but that was authenticated by a missionary. At the confrontation of Kapi'olani and a priestess of Pele in 1824, the priestess drew forth a piece of tapa with symbols on it and began to "read" it to the group. After Kapi'olani looked at the paper, she tried to grab it away and, failing to do so, she denounced it as a fraud.

More and more evidence is being accumulated which tends to indicate that the petroglyphs were a kind of writing utilized by the kāhuna for special purposes, perhaps as a means of recording names. An intensive, open minded study might reveal that the Hawaiians were indeed literate.

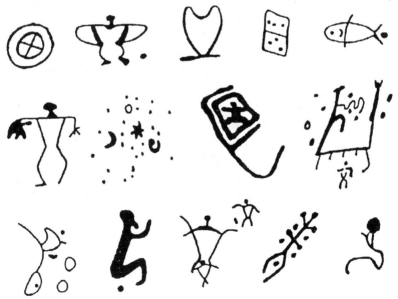

Petroglyphs at Pu'uloa, Hawai'i

HEALERS

In no field were the kāhuna more advanced than in that of medicine. At the time that most European doctors were bleeding patients with dirty hands, the Hawaiian medical kāhuna were dealing successfully with ulcers, heart trouble, epilepsy and cancer. Some of the practices of two hundred years ago have a surprising similarity to those in our world today. The cost of curing was high, and unless he was important or wealthy, the patient was not brought to the doctor. Inevitably, too, the doctor rebuked those who used home remedies first before seeking outside help (e 'imi i ka ola mawako).

The routine medical procedure was fairly modern as well. The kāhuna lapa'au examined the patient and either diagnosed the malady or sent him to a specialist who could do this. If the illness was one that the kahuna could treat, he prescribed medicine for a number of days, ordered the amount and kind of rest or activity, restricted the diet to certain foods or fluids and ordained the kind of purge necessary to rid the system of medication and wastes of the sickness as an end to the therapy.

Internal ailments were treated by the administration of herb mixtures, extractions from sea animals and a few inorganic substances, rather than abdominal operations. Their most delicate surgery apparently was the removal of cataracts from the eye, using the razor sharp edge of a certain kind of grass. To what extent the kāhuna practiced trepanning is difficult to determine. It is claimed that attempts were made to replace damaged portions of the cranium with perfectly fitted pieces of coconut shell or bone sections taken from other human skulls. Minor surgical techniques included a kind of circumcision, lancing of boils and infections, and abortions.

Many old Hawaiian medical practices antedated those of modern medicine by hundreds of years. 'Awa, a soporific which works on the spinal cord, was used as a tranquilizer and, in cases of obesity, used to curb the appetite. The root was also utilized to treat enuresis and insomnia. Morning-glory root (koali)

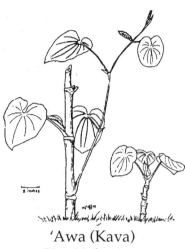

'Awa (Kava)
Piper Methysticum

was employed as a counterirritant for sprains, broken bones and dislocations while its heat-engendering qualities made it ideal to treat arthritis and rheumatism. Arrowroot starch (pia) was administered for internal bleeding and diarrhea. Salt water was given immediately to someone in shock, used to cleanse wounds and taken as a mild laxative by the aged. 'Alaea, a natural water soluble iron oxide, was given to any who suffered loss of blood, to women with excessive menses, and to patients who were abnormally tired or had loss of appetite. Frequent application of turtle oil (honu hinu) over a period of time was used to erase scars that were not pitted and to remove unwanted lines from the face and neck. One of the treatments of puncture wounds and some sores called for a poultice of material taken from a particular horizon of the organic layer of the soil and applied directly to the injury. This may have been a primitive method of taking advantage of the antibiotics in organic earth.

Some of the old procedures of medication were in perfect keeping with the principles of hygiene taught in schools today. The seriously ill were often placed in isolation in a small house expressly built for the purpose and which, when its usefulness was ended, was destroyed. If possible, the injured were treated on the spot and if bleeding occurred, it was stopped by a compress or styptic and the wound left exposed to the air which permitted more rapid recovery.

The foregoing are easily understandable in the light of modern methods while the following remain equally obscure. Some mental aberrations were treated by periodically forcing the patient to abstain from solid foods, while others were stuffed with a decoction of fern. Certain disorders were diagnosed by smelling the bed, the breath or the excretions of the patient or by watching the kind of insects attracted by the urine or the spittle. A preponderance of medication included a laxative or an enema even though the malady might be external.

Among most primitive peoples, the same medicine man or witch doctor handled everything from placating the gods to curing the sick whether they were possessed by devils or had obvious injuries. This was not the case in the civilized society of Hawai'i. The medical profession was not only set apart but in turn was divided into many groups with recognized specialists in each category. A few of those which correspond roughly with medical careers today are listed below.

Kāhuna lā'au lapa'au	—	pharmacologists and general practitioners
Kāhuna lomilomi	—	physiotherapists, masseurs
Kāhuna hāhā	—	diagnosticians
Kāhuna koholua	—	surgeons (minor surgery)
Kāhuna ha'i'wi	—	bone specialists
Kāhuna ho'ohānau	—	obstetricians

The kāhuna ho'ohānau will serve to illustrate some of the diverse abilities of the Hawaiian medical specialist. At the time these islands were being explored by Captain Cook, men as obstetric physicians were just beginning to be accepted in Europe. (Many civilized countries were able to resist "male midwives" for more than a century after that.) In Hawai'i, however, the kāhuna ho'ohānau, or child delivering specialist, had long been a part of the native way of life. This master could deal with all of the exigencies of childbirth and, if he wished, could assure the mother a painless experience while he assumed the travail himself. At times, in what some will find a poetic justice, the kahuna would take the labor pains from the mother and transfer them to the father who would writhe in agony for a lengthy period while his wife barely sensed the contractions. Often this specialist not only was in attendance at parturition but had charge of the prenatal and postnatal care as well, regulating the diet, condition and activity of mother and child.

Ideally, the birthing expert might also be a specialist in latent childhood diseases (kāhuna hāhā pā'ao'au). When the child was delivered, it was cleaned and examined thoroughly all over. Particular attention was given to the investigation of hands and feet. The kahuna would study closely the fingers and toes as well and then be able to announce that the child in later years would have a propensity toward this or that disease or affliction. One of the things looked for was the fine tracing of blood vessels on the baby's abdomen ('ōpūlauoho). According to Mary Pukui, these tracings, which vanished shortly after birth, indicated that a male child would grow up to be sterile or, if the infant was female, that it would not have offspring that lived more than a few months.

Unfortunately, too little remains of the practices of the trained medical kāhuna, and some of the knowledge that has been handed down has been altered by the use of introduced plants such as tobacco, melons and peppers. Some treatments which are extant today are undoubtedly old and have been kept intact perhaps because they have been used often and because they still work.

Stone Pounder
(3" high x 1½" wide)

A few of the old Hawaiian medicines are being examined by physicians and technicians today in the search for new solutions to old medical problems. One such "discovery" is said to be an anti-cancer serum extracted from the tentacles of sea worms. Once a part of an ancient Hawaiian remedy, it now holds a promise of being a cure for cancer. Although it has only been tested on laboratory animals, the results are reputed to be good in arresting certain kinds of carcinoma.

One of the difficulties that modern researchers meet is the reluctance of the aged Hawaiians to share the secrets handed down through the generations. It has been important for a family to keep intact certain remedies since a lineage may have a particular affliction crop out every generation or two. Many of these formulae have been passed on with the kapu that they may not be used or given outside the family. Others may be related but never written down, while some unrestricted ones are guarded lest someone profit by the bones of the ancestors.

A few of the people in possession of medicinal recipes have relented and released the information because of concern that soon some or all of the necessary plants may be exterminated or altered by the spread of modern civilization. There are more persons, however, who will carry their secrets to the grave for purely personal reasons.

Who can blame the old people for withholding information about Hawaiian medicine when in the past the foreign doctors have openly ridiculed the very data they solicited without first testing it? A lecturer devoted a greater part of an evening lampooning Hawaiian medical practices only to end his talk with a plea for those who had some of the old formulas to surrender them to scientific scrutiny.

One Hawaiian woman claims that once, after she was asked to detail some old treatments involving mixtures of plant materials, she was told that some of the ingredients had been already tried and found to be of no use. Her questioners said that they never checked combinations because, in their experience with native medicines in other countries, only one or two of the constituents were ever active and that the rest were used to conceal them. (According to our agreement the following is also included.) She said, "Tell them this is Hawai'i, not just a country.[sic] These are the same kind of people who ask me how to make my good laulau and then change beef for pig, and spinach for taro leaves, leave out butterfish and cook in foil instead of lā'ī and then tell others it doesn't taste like mine because I gave them a wrong recipe!"

Perhaps such antagonistic encounters as this have done a great deal toward erecting a barrier as formidable as the kapu between the researchers and the people of Hawai'i.

Although hundreds of medicinal plants were available in the pharmacopoeia of the islands, the kāhuna did not rely on them alone. Just as today, the medical men of old recognized that the psyche and the soma are inseparable and that malfunction of the body can disturb the mind and that fears, frustrations and mental uncertainties affect the well being of the physical system. As a consequence, he treated the entire man with all the tools of physiotherapy and psychotherapy at his command. Because the diagnosis and treatment were guided by the gods and the complainer had an unwavering faith in the doctor, the medication and the spirits involved, many otherwise miraculous cures were effected. Even when the patient was a foreigner with no comprehension of the Hawaiian language or medical methods, the results were sometimes remarkable.

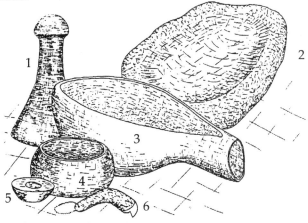

Some Medicinal Tools of old Hawai'i
1. Stone Pounder 2. Stone Salt Pan 3. Gourd Strainer
4. Wood Bowl 5. Stone Kāhuna Cup 6. Shark Tooth Knife

Hilo in 1860. *Woodcut by K. Johnson*

The Man Who Moved Too Fast

In the winter of 1856, a small sailing vessel enroute from Maui to the Big Island of Hawai'i, dropped anchor in Hilo Bay. Strong kona winds had prevented the captain from making port in Kailua on the western side of the island but two of his passengers couldn't have been happier about their circumstance.

One was Caleb Thompson, a young man from Massachusetts. The other youth was a Hawaiian called Keone, whose home was Waiākea, scarcely a rifle shot away from the anchored ship. It seemed like providence that the brig had come to Hilo, saving them a long difficult journey around half the island. The two had become friends at Lahaina, although Keone wasn't sure how long the relationship would last because Caleb had a wasting sickness. He was thin to the point of being only skin and bone, always tired and trembled like an 'ōlapa in the slightest wind.

One of the first things that Keone did after his family had greeted them was to find out where his mother's uncle was living.

"He is very old but there is no better doctor anywhere," Keone told Caleb. "Before long he will have you as strong and healthful as I am."

Caleb was frankly skeptical. He had visited many of the medical men in New England. One by one they had shaken their bearded heads and informed him that his malady, whatever it was, was incurable. Finally, he gave up going to doctors at all and decided to take an ocean voyage, less to see the world than to escape the pity showered on him by his friends and relatives. He had little hope to find a cure in Hawai'i but, if it pleased his companion, he would go to see the uncle.

A few days later, Keone took his new chum to visit the family kahuna. The old man was quite unlike any doctor that Caleb had ever seen or even heard about. He wore only a pair of trousers and a garland of green grass which passed around his scrawny neck and hung almost to his belt. His office was the convenient shade of a kou tree nearby his shack. The old kahuna listened to what Keone told him, then smelled Caleb's breath and began a fingertip exploration of the young man's emaciated body. When the examination ended, the old man sat for a long time staring at some point on Caleb's neck. Finally he spoke, but with no gestures and little change of facial expression, so that Caleb found it impossible to even guess what was being said in Hawaiian.

When the kahuna finished speaking, Keone began to translate. "My mother's uncle says that you yet may live. If you do not change your ways, though, you will surely die. You have moved much too fast for a long time and have left a part of yourself behind. Now you must slow down so that part of yourself may catch up. You must not just lie about, however, or your other part will have no eagerness to join you, but you must look around and when you find something new you

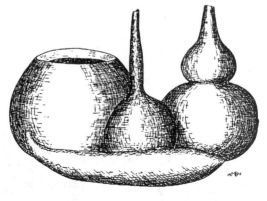

Hawaiian Gourds

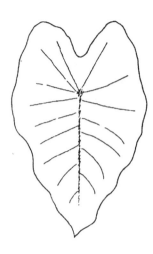

Kalo Leaf (Lū'au)

must say aloud, 'Look, I have found a thing I have never known before!' This will make your other part want to join you. The more often you say this the better it will be.

At every opportunity, you must eat lū'au with red salt, for these are the things that your other part craves. By eating them in abundance you will encourage your other part to join you and stay with you. He says that he will pray for you and will pray also that you heed his words."

Because of the old man's prescription, Keone took Caleb to visit one relative after another. They leisurely toured the coast of Puna and everywhere they stopped the young foreigner was given his fill of green taro leaves.

Almost a year later, they reached the Ka'ū district and traveled on slowly toward the southern point of the island. By that time, the kahuna's advice had taken visible effect. Caleb no longer shook and had begun to fill out his skin, which had darkened considerably in the summer sun. It was in Ka'ū that the cure became complete, for Caleb met a beautiful Hawaiian girl and, after a suitable courtship, made her his wife.

After a time, the newlyweds went to the booming land of California where Caleb went into business, raised a family and lived to an old age. This was the great, great grandfather of Mrs. Jean Thompson Foster, who told this story one chilly day on a beach not far from San Francisco.

OTHER PROFESSIONS

*V*irtually every field of endeavor in the islands had a kahuna who, as both master and teacher, perpetuated a certain portion of the culture of old Hawai'i. Some of the monumental works of rock which remain today testify to the prowess of the ancient engineers who devised the means of moving and placing boulders of exceptional size and tonnage. The burial caves (anahūnā) of great chiefs are said to be guarded by huge blocks of basalt which have been engineered to fall or slide when triggered by an intruder. Stone sled courses (hōlua), as long and steep as ski jumps, still manifest the careful planning and execution of such slides.

Some of the oldest stone works are the artificial fish ponds created for the practice of aquaculture. It was the duty of certain specialists to breed and raise fish to provide a never failing supply of seafood for the chiefs. Kāhuna of a related profession regulated the fishing seasons and established temporary conservation areas where sea animals and plants could flourish untouched. After a suitable time, these enclosures were opened to use and neighboring shores were made out of bounds.

Highly qualified architects (kuhikuhipu'uone) designed and constructed the temples of old, building smooth faced walls and platforms without mortar which were capable of supporting large structures and images. The ability of the Hawaiian architect was demonstrated to the foreigners during the missionary period on the Big Island. In the early 1800's, a huge timber framed building accommodating 2,000 persons was erected in Hilo. Thatching of the edifice alone was estimated to have weighed several tons.

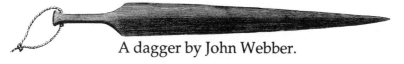

A dagger by John Webber.

Shark Tooth
Studded Club
by John Webber

A part of a chief's retinue consisted of kāhuna versed in the military arts of fighting with spears, daggers, staffs, clubs, tripping and noosing weapons, and the science of deadly unarmed combat (lua). Also attached to the court of important chiefs were professional historians, genealogists, counselors, surveyors and entertainers, although some of the latter were in traveling troupes which followed the professional tax collectors around the island during the Makahiki festival season. These were the acrobats, jugglers, puppet masters and storytellers, to mention a few.

Making the same circuit as the entertainers were experts in boxing, pole vaulting, wrestling, throwing and many sports of rolling stone discs and balls as well as a multitude of games of all kinds. Any tournament or competition drew vast crowds of spectators eager to bet on the outcome. Professional gamblers who might not wager for themselves were often available for amateurs to consult. They shrewdly calculated the odds in sports and contests and combatted the evil spirits (aumiha) thought to attend the games.

One sport in which every man considered himself a master was that of cock fighting. Some trained their birds to dodge, feint and strike by using smoke, some by tossing pebbles, a few by using a decoy and others by means which they never revealed.

Chicken Petroglyph

SORCERERS

$\mathscr{A}$nything written concerning the kāhuna must neces-
sarily include something about sorcery. Unfortunately, with
the passage of time, it has assumed an importance today that
it may not have had in times past. More has been printed
about sorcery than any other phase of the mystical practices
of the Hawaiian priesthood. For the most part, it deals with
the use of spirits to cause illness or death to someone who
has willingly or unwittingly offended a kahuna or his em-
ployer. It is these stories which have given both residents and
visitors the concept of complete evil concerning the kāhuna.
If only a fraction of these tales were true, it would still leave
a vast number of unexplained incidents to baffle the scientist
and researcher.

Even more puzzling to many are the feats of magic which
have been attributed to the priests of old. The students of
sorcery studied in a house (moku hale) well removed from
any other structures. There they learned how to tap the power
of the infinite to obtain extraordinary abilities ('e'epa), how
to gain spiritual aid and learned a kind of deep insight ('ike
kūhohonu). Their training was lengthy, but when all phases
were completed and the graduation ceremony ('ūniki) held,
the new sorcerers could concentrate (kia) on a cliff causing it
to crumble and make trees some distance away burst into
flame.

Perhaps none of the modern kāhuna can do these things
but according to common belief, some have considerable ability. Only a generation or two ago a few could be found who
had the faculty of fire walking (paulā'ī). Within the past few
decades, things have been witnessed which are difficult to
explain by commonly accepted natural principles.

A few years ago, several Hawaiian men were preparing
to kālua a pig in an imu. The earth oven had been uncovered

Meeting Place of an Ancient Secret Society. (from a painting in the Royal Palace)

revealing an interior shimmering with heat. A number of rounded, fist-sized stones had been removed from the ashes and one of the workmen was dipping his hand in a pan of water, then selecting from the pile of hot rocks and bare-handed stuffing the internal cavity of the pig. When he was asked how he could hold such an obviously scorching piece of lava for that long, he merely laughed and picked up another. This time he held it out palm up while he chanted softly in Hawaiian. After holding the stone for a minute or more, he dropped it into the pan of water causing it to hiss with steam. Then without a word he went back to filling the pig with the rest of the hot stones.

More recently, men of advanced years have performed feats of strength considered remarkable for any age and others have demonstrated their talent to assemble a multitude of sharks by simply chanting at the edge of the sea. Some are still thought to possess the prayers of death but few dare admit having the gift because such sorcery is against the law.

According to S.M. Kamakau, even in old Hawai'i the practice of praying to death was frowned upon by many priests and most of the people. Though a kahuna learned the art of destruction, he was supposed to control his temper, covet nothing belonging to others and leave vengeance to the gods. One who was thought to abuse his aptitude for 'anā'anā was called a filth eater ('aihamu) or a murdering kahuna and at times some were put to death for slaying others for their own gain. Nevertheless, the practice of death dealing was taught and fostered by the priesthood perhaps as a defense against those who organized against them.

If a righteous reason existed for the actions of some "killing kāhuna" perhaps it can be found in something that has scarcely been examined. Men's societies existed in Hawai'i as they did in other cultures throughout the world. One such club restricted the membership to those who owned a feather cloak and, in all likelihood, the canoemen wearing the gourd masks (mākini) in the famous drawing made by John Webber at the time of Captain Cook's voyage, belonged to another. This sort of thing might be the foundation of the stories in which the kahuna is pitted against a man capable of chang-

A Canoe of the Sandwich Islands, the Rowers Masked

ing into a shark. Hawaiian legend is replete with tales such as the following told to William Rice.

"Near the waterhole of Malaekahana between Lā'ie and Kahuku, lived a man call Manō-niho-kahi who was possessed of the power to turn himself into a shark. Manō appeared as other men except that he always wore a tapa cloth which concealed the shark mouth on his back.

"Whenever he saw women going to the sea to fish or get limu, he would call out, 'Are you going into the sea to fish?' Upon hearing that they were, he would hasten in a roundabout way to reach the sea, where he would come upon them and, biting them with his own shark's tooth, kill them.

"This happened many times. Many women were killed by Manō. At last the chief of the region became alarmed and ordered all the people to gather together on the plain. Standing with his kahuna, the chief commanded all the people to disrobe. All obeyed but Manō-niho-kahi, Shark-with-one-tooth. So his kapa was dragged off and there on his back was seen the shark's mouth. He was put to death at once and there were no more deaths among the women."

Manō ~ Shark

In most of the stories, the shark-man seeks out the kahuna and engages him in a contest with the life of the loser forfeit. Invariably, the cloak of the priest's antagonist is torn away exposing the shark mouth (a tattoo?) and he is put to death. Perhaps the priesthood felt that anti-kāhuna organizations such as these were a grave threat and thus when a member was discovered, his praying to death was justified.

Praying to death is often explained as the use of suggestion on the untutored minds of the natives or the administration of poisons, some of which might be presently unknown to forensic medicine. Neither of these explanations can be discounted, but at the same time neither are necessary according to the kāhuna. Although the most accomplished of the death dealers was Hawa'e who lived near Kailua, Kona on Hawai'i, it is generally acceded that Moloka'i was the place famous (wahi pana) for the "senders of destruction."

Gourd Masks

THE SIX STICKS

In the early 1900's, grass houses were already becoming uncommon in Hawai'i. On the southern shore of Moloka'i, not far from a village, was a thatched structure of ancient age. Nobody remembered when it was built. It had always been there. Apparently, it was the home of an equally old man who was never seen to do anything but sit on a pile of mats and gaze at the sea. No one had ever seen him fishing, tending a garden or employed at any work. He had no visitors. His occupation was simply watching the ocean. How he kept alive no one knew or cared, for the talk was that he was once a kahuna of great power. When going by the old man's kuleana was unavoidable, it was considered wise to look neither left nor right, but to keep the eyes on the path lest one

step upon a cross mark or kī leaves which would bring misfortune.

The old man might never have been disturbed for the
length of his days had it not been for the effects of alcohol.
By chance, one day, a young man named Lopaka and his
friends wandered in that direction. They were celebrating
payday and their new wealth by passing a quart of 'ōkolehao
among themselves as they meandered up the beach engaged
with jokes and good-natured horseplay.

The bottle was nearly empty when one of the young men
glanced up and saw the old man seated in front of his house
looking right at them. The youth gestured wildly at his com-
panions and whispered that they had to go back now. All
quickly agreed except Lopaka who declared that he wasn't
afraid of the 'elemakule and proved it by staggering toward
the house, holding out the bottle.

"Here, old man," called Lopaka, "take the last drink. It
will rest your eyes and change your day."

If the aged Hawaiian heard, he gave no indication but
continued to sit cross-legged on the mats. His kīhei and malo
were of clean tapa and across his lap was a thin stick with a
tuft of dog hair tied to the end. Thinking the old fellow hard

Ti or Kī

of hearing, Lopaka repeated the invita-
tion in a shout, but still got no response.

Angered by the ancient one's indifference, Lopaka drained the bottle
and threw it on the ground. Then he
grabbed up the old kahuna's stick and
snapped it into six pieces. For the first
time, the figure on the mats moved.
From under the kīhei came a long bony
arm that raked up the fragments and
deftly lined them up in the sand at the
edge of the mat.

In a low, clear voice, the old man
addressed Lopaka. "Each stick is a day.
Tomorrow I will remove one. The next
day another. When all the sticks are
gone, you will die."

Lopaka roared with laughter, "Speak of your own end, old man, for you are nearer the grave than I am." He then kicked the sticks away and still chuckling, lurched down the strand to join his friends who were rapidly leaving him behind.

By the following day, the story had spread throughout the countryside and many people came to Lopaka's house to offer advice and sympathy to his parents. At their urging, the father decided to go to the old sorcerer to ask what reparation could be made for his son's transgression. He thought about the problem all night and by morning had chosen his words and the goods that he would offer. He found the old man seated as always but with only four sticks left standing in the sand in front of him. Though he promised many things, not a word or movement answered the father's request and so he returned home.

Lopaka's mother tried the next day, but she found that a woman's tears had no more effect than the arguments of a father and she was even more distressed because only three sticks were left.

When Lopaka himself returned to the old man's place, just two sticks remained to decorate the sand. For the sake of his parents, he begged and pleaded for his life, saying that he was sorry and promising to do anything within reason to make up for the wrong he had committed. As before, his words fell on deaf ears and Lopaka returned to his home a completely changed young man.

"There is not any need for you to worry more," Lopaka told his parents, "nor will you have to plan a funeral, for I have decided to go away so that the works of the old man will not concern us."

Lopaka ate a hasty meal prepared by his mother, while his father gathered a few necessities for his trip and with a brief aloha he left the land of his birth.

Two days later, he was found on another island, sprawled on the beach in death, with a short broken stick clutched tightly in his fist.

THE POWER OF WORDS

$\mathscr{A}$ key to the secret of the mystical abilities of the kāhuna may be their belief in the power of words. They are no longer entirely alone in this persuasion, for modern science has discovered that words may have a potency beyond mere communication. The very name of the place one lives can seemingly have an influence on the individual over and above other considerations. Computer technology has revealed the puzzling coincidence that people with the same names often share common personality traits.

The priests of old Hawai'i would have been surprised by our reluctance to accept these principles. Their feeling on the significance of place names has already been mentioned in the section on accomplishments. They apparently placed even more importance on another phase of the language arts. The priesthood discovered very early in its history that the full force of word power could be realized by the careful composition and rendering of prayers. During their years of training, the priests learned the rituals and prayers handed down faithfully from the past. They were considered accomplished only when they could produce all they had committed without hesitation or effort (walewaha).

The wisest men in old Hawai'i had no doubts concerning the power of prayer. Their spiritual attendant ('aumakua) was always with them forming the link between themselves and the infinite. Being thus constantly in touch with an uninhibited strength beyond their own, the deeds, words and gestures of the kāhuna were able to cause things to be done. Their prayers were the focus of force emanating from their being, perhaps from the conscious and subconscious mind and properly rendered were as effective for their purpose as a spear thrown in battle.

The above analogy is a good one, for the spear is a prayer

(pule), the aim is concentration (kia), the strength of cast is desire (kuko), the direction is the objective (mākia), confidence in ability is faith (paulele) and the lack of wind is no distraction (malukia). Just as all spears do not find their target in warfare, however, not all prayers command results either. Any of the former factors might be wanting or a new element might be introduced which could necessitate fundamental changes.

Of the mystical constituents in accomplishing a purpose through the power of words, desire was considered the most important. Intense desire might brush aside obstacles, make them inconsequential or even pierce them to achieve ambition. It was important, therefore, to keep desire high by fixing the mind often on the objective. This was much easier if the purpose was to gain something material. Often, however, the desired end was something abstract which could not be pictured. Then the kahuna selected something material which had a name coincident with the abstract thought and used it as an objective reminder.

A good example of this word power symbolism is found in the selection of offerings for the ritual of love magic (hana aloha). The āhole fish was offered because the name contains hole which means to strip away. Indifference must be stripped away before love can be inspired.

Lele was the banana offered to secure divine aid because the essence was thought to fly (lele) to the gods. The sugar cane pili mai was used because pili means to cling or hold fast, a desirable attribute of beginning affection. If the hana aloha sought to bring back an errant love then the sea cucumber (loli) and the kāmole plant were used. Loli also means to change and kamole also means to return as after estrangement. These abstract offerings strengthened the love prayer (kuoha) and rendered the priest's work efficacious, although induced love was never as strong or as satisfactory as the natural kind. Those under the spell had glazed eyes and became childlike, demonstrating little interest for anything beyond the object of fixation.

Words were often considered no less strong than deeds themselves. If, for example, a special house was needed immediately but there was no time to build one, the kahuna quickly conducted the final ceremony of the building dedication, announced that the structure was entirely done and went on to the next phase of the ritual.

When time permitted, the priesthood of old Hawai'i could accomplish virtually anything. Faced with a particularly formidable task, they might apply their efforts in concert like batteries in a series to create a common desire that was overwhelming. At certain times, they gathered this way in secret to pray for a chief ('ahamaka).

If you would like to test for yourself a part of the word power of the kāhuna, select something material that you would like to have. Try to pick a thing beyond your means but not too much so in order to develop your ability and confidence by initial success. Print the name of the object on a card and put it where you can see it often. Each time you see the name, visualize it as much as your imagination permits until your desire for it becomes very strong. Repeat this every day until your want becomes a reality. In so doing, you will have used an instrument which has been discovered and rediscovered many times in the history of man and one which was a portion of the hidden knowledge of the kāhuna.

Kahuna may be derived from two words, ka huna, literally, the secret. Another division of the word gives kahu na, a guardian or keeper of something. Thus, in its entirety, the word kahuna has been interpreted as meaning the guardian of the secret.

The secret is still guarded today, although it has been said that if it was openly revealed, it would not be believed anyhow. It seems likely that the secret deals with the method that was used by the kāhuna to attain the knowledge and power which lie beyond man through spiritual insight and faith.

Some believe that the successes of the priests were due to their ability to trap and enslave disassociated spirits ('unihipili) and use them for sorcery, defined as the use of power gained from the assistance or control of evil spirits. The spiritual aides employed in old Hawai'i were seldom evil but convention dictates the use of the word to cover the myriads of otherwise unexplainable accomplishments of the kāhuna.

A man in a kī leaf cape (ahu lā'i) carrying 'umeke.

IN CONCLUSION

*O*nly a few decades ago in Hawai'i, almost every ground breaking, dedication or open house of importance featured an ancient ceremony presided over by a kahuna. This picturesque person, often draped in a white robe and garlanded with a maile lei, sprinkled a bit of water with a kī leaf and, in Hawaiian, blessed the land, banning evil influence from the designated area for all time. At the more elaborate ceremonies, the kahuna might have an attendant who carried the small calabash of holy water and perhaps another who began and ended the performance with a soft note on a shell trumpet.

If an unreasonable number of accidents occurred during the construction of a road or a building in those days, it was not uncommon for the workers to walk off the job until a kahuna came to clear away the cause of the misfortune.

More and more in functions like these, the kāhuna is being supplanted by clergy of conventional faiths who wear street attire and may or may not say a few words in Hawaiian. Within the foreseeable future, this last reminder of the native priesthood may pass into oblivion.

How much of the knowledge of earlier times has been handed down to these days is difficult to judge. It may be that far more has been passed along than we can imagine. When the kapu system fell in 1819, the organized religion of old was set aside and the orders of priests disbanded. So far as is known, no provision was made to insure that the ability and knowledge of the kāhuna would not be lost when the priests of that time died. They were, in fact, under a kapu never to reveal the secrets of the order. Perhaps the ban permitted some things to be taught to younger relatives, for some of the old knowledge seems to have been perpetuated. Some reputed as kāhuna today must have a measure of the old abilities, gained perhaps as a family inheritance.

ADDITIONS and CORRECTIONS — 1983
by L.R. McBride

$\mathscr{W}$ithin the last decade, since this book was first published, it has received some criticism. Most was constructive but a few of the knowledgeable old people have felt that some things in the book should never have been mentioned. Although I agree in part, to remove them now would call attention to the omissions and emphasize their importance.

Time alone has changed a few things. The Star of the Sea Church in the village of Kalapana no longer has a painting of Pā'ao among its decorations. This is a loss that perhaps only a few can comprehend. In 1974, the new penal code enacted by the State of Hawaii no longer condemns the kāhuna (see Year 2000 Additions). A person may now practice openly those things suppressed by law for a century and a half, including sorcery. Anyone may now claim to be a kahuna even if they have had no training, do not understand the Hawaiian language and have but slight or no knowledge of the ancient practices.

Some of the suggestions offered have been truly helpful to anyone interested in the educational system of pre-historic Hawai'i. It has now been corroborated that talented children were chosen from the ranks of both the ruling class (ali'i) and the commoners (maka'āinana) and once picked, rank and class were considered less important than scholastic ability. Likewise, little difference was made between sexes and it is suggested that the preponderance of males was due to the reluctance of the females to give up their freedom for the rigid discipline of some schools. Children just old enough to hold a coconut in each hand were selected by a master chooser (kahuna mōae) on the basis of ability, intelligence and desire. The boys and girls that were picked learned the fundamentals needed for all disciplines; a kind of mathematics which included counting, measuring, aspects of geometry and trigonometry, communication, the elements of anatomy of people and animals, the stars and constellations, the nature of the land and the sea, a kind of taxonomy of plants and the first stages of use of the power of the mind. After being observed for some time, the students were selected to attend specialized schools of instruction (hālau).

The ancient Hawaiian educational system had some similarities to colleges of today. Each hālau differed from that in a different place conducted by different instructors even though both taught the same subject. Some schools were thought to be better than others. Naturally, a graduate believed his school to be the best.

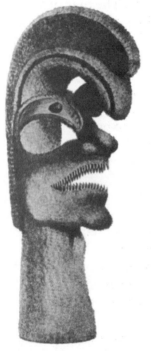

A'ole'oe, no kēia hālau.
No laila 'a'ole no oe
i 'ike i ko'u po'opo'o.

You are not of my school.
Therefore you cannot know
the depths of my understanding.

Some things were completely different from present day systems of education. The social amenities of the time required that a kahuna mention his ultimate teacher in his introduction to any new place and whether that instructor still lived.

There is reason to believe that kāhuna were able to communicate not only in Hawaiian but by another "language" as well. The words had the same sounds but were unknown to the uneducated people. Mary Pukui includes a number of "kahuna words" in her dictionary. Some are directions, cardinal points of the compass, names of some plants, stars, rocks and tools. Whether these words, including those unrecorded, were enough to constitute a separate language is unknown.

From the time of Pā'ao, foreigners of rare ability and knowledge were accepted into the ranks of kāhuna. They could have brought new words to the educational system. This is probable but not necessary. Certainly the use of figurative speech among the educated would enable them to discuss any subject openly without others present comprehending.

A person had to complete a course of study and graduate ('ailolo). If they did not, they could never work even as an apprentice or a menial in that field of endeavor. If a student spent many years of life toward attaining mastery of a subject and quit, they seldom were content to face a life of piling rocks or tilling the soil. Many in such a circumstance used what they had learned to become sorcerers. Some "drop outs" became water seekers, self styled prophets, fortune tellers, luck makers, or workers of love magic and other relatively harmless activities. Some became workers of "black magic," using the power of the mind to cause illness or death to others for a price. The latter were scorned by true masters but few doubted their ability.

The kāhuna may be considered as a product of a remarkable and outstanding educational system. It is unfortunate that some of the missionaries equated kāhuna with priests similar to those found in other native cultures. They matched them with shaman, fakirs, and medicine men and supposed the kāhuna to mostly deal with religious and mystical matters. One missionary remarked that "in every village there seems to be several kāhuna to oppose us." This misunderstanding led the foreigners to persuade the kuhina nui, Ka'ahumanu, to banish the Hawaiian schools in 1828.

Although the kāhuna believed in the gods and especially in their tutelary deity, only one kind of kāhuna dealt particularly with religion. The kāhuna pule or praying professional led the people in matters of worship and in the rituals of dedication and purification. They were a small percentage of the learned class of men and women who had spent at least half of their life studying to become masters of an art, a craft, or a science.

L.R. McBride, March 1983

ᏓᏆ

BIBLIOGRAPHY

Alexander, W.D. ~ *A Brief History of the Hawaiian People*, 1891, New York

Beckwith, M.W. ~ *Hawaiian Mythology*, 1940, New Haven

Brinkley & Kikuchi ~ *History of the Japanese People*, 1915, New York

Degener, O. ~ *Plants of Hawaii National Park*, 1945, Ann Arbor

Diaz Del Castillo, B. ~ *Conquest of New Spain*, 1963, New York

Dibble, S. ~ *History of the Sandwich Islands*, 1909, Honolulu

Ellis, W. A. ~ *A Narrative of a Tour Through Hawaii*, 1917, Reprint London

Emerson, N.B. ~ *Unwritten Literature of Hawaii*, 1965, Reprint Tokyo

Fornander, A ~ *The Polynesian Race*, 1882, London

Fornander, A. ~ *Fornander Collection of Hawaiian Antiquities I-III*,
            Bernice P. Bishop Museum Memoirs, 1916-1920, Vols. 4, 5, 6

Hale'ole, S.N. ~ *History of the Hawaiian Priesthood*, 1862, 1863

'Ī'ī, John Papa ~ *Fragments of Hawaiian History*, 1959, Honolulu

Ka'aiakamanu & Akina ~ *Hawaiian Herbs*, translated by A. Akana, 1922,
            Honolulu

Kalakaua, David ~ *Legends and Myths of Hawaii*, 1888, New York

Kamakau, S.M. ~ *Ka Po'e Kahiko*, 1870, Reprint of Newspaper Ke Au 'Oko'a
            1964

Kamakau, S.M ~ *Ruling Chiefs of Hawai'i*, 1961, Honolulu

Malo, David ~ *Hawaiian Antiquities*, 1951, Bernice P.Bishop Musuem, Honolulu

McBride, Likeke R. ~ *Petroglyphs of Hawai'i*, Revised edition 1997, Hilo

Pearson, Richard (ed.) ~ *Archaeology on the Island of Hawaii*, 1969, Honolulu

Pukui, M.K. & Elbert, S.H. ~ *Hawaiian English Dictionary*, 1957, Honolulu

Rice, W.H. ~ *Hawaiian Legends*, 1923, B.P.Bishop Museum Bulletin 3

Thrum, T.G. ~ *"Heiaus and Heiau Sites"*, 1907, Hawaiian Annual, Honolulu

Additions and Corrections - Year 2000
by Andrew S. McBride

*A*s the old chant states, Pele the volcano goddess is capable of great destruction near the seashore.

The Star of the Sea Church (also known as the "Painted Church") was moved from Kalapana to a new location to prevent its destruction by lava flows from Pu'u 'Ō'ō vents on Kīlauea volcano. Kīlauea has been erupting continuously since January 1983. The site on which the Church stood has since been covered by lava. Kaimū black sand beach was destroyed in August 1990.

Waha'ula heiau has now been destroyed by lava flows from Pu'u 'Ō'ō also. Often threatened by flows from the vent, the famous heiau was completely destroyed by lava in August 1997.

In addition to Kaimū black sand beach and Waha'ula heiau, a number of archaeological and historic sites have been destroyed by the eruption. These include Queen's Bath, Kamoamoa sites including petroglyphs, and much of the former village of Kalapana.

Pele continues to build what will become a new island someday far in the future. Lō'ihi is the name of the seamount, an active volcano growing from the hot spot in the earth's crust. It was recently estimated that the seamount's summit is "about 3,154 feet below the ocean's surface."

A minor correction with additional clarification is needed for a paragraph concerning the legal status of the kāhuna. In 1983, my father, Likeke McBride, wrote:

> In 1974, the new penal code enacted by the State of Hawai'i no longer condemns the kāhuna. A person may now practice openly those things suppressed by law for a century and a half, including

sorcery. Anyone may now claim to be a kahuna
even if they have had no training, do not understand the Hawaiian language and have but slight
or no knowledge of the ancient practices.

The new penal code enacted by the State of Hawai'i was
effective January 1, 1973. Otherwise, the first sentence is a
true statement. The new penal code repealed the sections
criminalizing and penalizing kahuna practices such as sorcery. The second and third sentences are statements made by
Likeke R. McBride concerning the implications of the repealed
laws.

I found no references to kahuna or sorcery in the current,
effective statutes (including the penal code) in my research
in Hawai'i law. It is interesting to survey the evolution of the
law concerning sorcery in Hawai'i.

In the Revised Laws of Hawai'i,1905, Chapter 89, Section
1077 with the heading "Sorcery, etc., penalty" read as fol-
lows:

> Any person who shall attempt the cure of another
> by practice of sorcery, witchcraft, anaana,
> hoopiopio, hoounauna, hoomanamana, or other
> superstitious or deceitful methods, shall, upon con-
> viction thereof, be fined in a sum not less than one
> hundred dollars, nor more than two hundred dol-
> lars or be imprisoned at hard labor not to exceed
> six months.

Additionally, in Chapter 221, Section 3195, those "who
practice hoopiopio, hoounauna, hoomanamana, anaana or
pretend to have the power of praying persons to death" were
included in the definition of vagrants and disorderly persons.

Significantly, these statutes quoted above remained in effect through the end of 1972, until the new penal code re-
pealing them was effective January 1,1973. While these statutes were renumbered and occasionally reworded, the text
remained remarkably similar over the years.

In the Revised Laws of 1935, the section "vagrants, disorderly persons, loitering" was expanded to include kāhuna, essentially criminalizing not only sorcery but also all kahuna practitioners. This statute remained the same in the Revised Laws of 1945.

In the Revised Laws of 1955, while "sorcery" was retained in the chapter heading, the word "kahunas" was deleted from the subsection title. With deletion of the word "kahunas" (on the books for 20 years), the implication exists that kāhuna were once again legal, at least as long as they did not practice sorcery. Indeed, Nadine Wharton reported in a 1965 article that Daddy Bray was honored in 1959 as "Hawai'i's Only Living Kahuna" by State Legislature resolution, implying legality and acceptance.

As mentioned above, the Hawai'i State penal code was made effective January 1, 1973. The penal code was issued as Title 37. Chapter 772 (concerning "vagrants, beggars, loiterers, sorcery") of the old Statutes was repealed and the provisions were not transfered. With the new penal code and repeal of Chapter 772, the practice of sorcery became theoretically legal.

Me ka pono,
Andrew S. McBride

Bay & Village of Hilo,
from the Hawaiian Gazette, 1890

Bibliography for Foreword
and Additions and Corrections - 2000

MAGAZINE AND NEWSPAPER ARTICLES:

~Gordon, Mike. *"Kahuna blesses Mighty Mo for voyage"* and *'A fair wind and a following sea.'* Honolulu Advertiser, May 23,1998, p. Al.

~Hewett, Frank K. *"Kāhuna tradition should decide,"* (letter to the editor), Honolulu Advertiser, March 30,1994, p. A16.

~Honolulu Advertiser (in general)

~Honolulu Star-Bulletin (in general)

~Johnson, Rubellite K. *"Rightful caretakers are Kawananakoa family,"* (letter to the editor), Honolulu Advertiser, March 30,1994, p. A16.

~Wharton, Nadine. *"Last of the Red-Hot Kahunas,"* Paradise of the Pacific, Vol. 77, number 12 (December,1965), p.112.

BOOKS:

~Chun, Malcolm Nāea, translator and editor. *Must We Wait in Despair: The 1867 Report of the 'Ahahui La'au Lapa'au of Wailuku, Maui on Native Hawaiian Health.* Honolulu: First People's Productions, 1994.

~Chun, Malcolm Nāea. *Nā Kukui Pio 'Ole, the Inextinguishable Torches: The Biographies of Three Early Hawaiian Scholars Davida Malo, S.N. Hale'ole and S. M. Kamakau.* Honolulu: First People's Productions,1993.

~Pukui, Mary Kawena. *'Olelo No'eau: Hawaiian Proverbs and Poetical Sayings.* Honolulu: Bishop Museum Press,1983.

~Pukui, Mary Kawena & Elbert, Samuel K. *Hawaiian Dictionary.* .Honolulu: UH Press,1986.

~Revised Laws of Hawai'i (RLH), 1905. Section 1077, p. 471; Section 3195, pp.1151-2.

~RLH, 1915. Section 1026, p. 465; Section 4199, p.1474.

~RLH, 1925. Section 1034, p. 468; Section 4492, p.1485.

~RLH, 1935. Section 1213, p. 224; Section 6310, p. 928.

~RLH, 1945. Section 11771, pp.1513-4; Section 11774, p.1514.

~RLH, 1955. Chapter 314-1, p.1555; Chapter 314-6, p.1556.

~Hawai'i Revised Statutes, 1968. Section 772-1, pp. 885-6; Section 772-6, p. 888.

~Hawai'i Revised Statutes. Special Supplement: Title 37, Hawai'i Penal Code Chapters 701-713. Table of Disposition, p. 326.

GLOSSARY

'Anā'anā	Evil sorcery.
Heiau	A place of worship
Imu	An underground oven.
Kahu	A guardian, keeper or honored attendant.
Kalo (Taro)	The cooked corms were mashed into poi, the Hawaiian staff of life.
Kālua	To bake in the underground oven.
Kapa (Tapa)	Paper cloth made from the inner bark of certain trees.
Kapu	Taboo, forbidden, consecrated.
Kī (Ti)	*Cordyline terminalis.* Frequently a thin un-branched stem topped with a cluster of oblong leaves up to two feet in length.
Kīhei	A rectangular kapa garment worn as a cloak.
Kou	*Cordia subcordata.* A tree once common near the sea, now rare.
Kukui	*Aleurites moluccana.* The candlenut tree.
Kuleana	A small piece of property.
Lā'ī	Kī leaf. Contraction of lau kī.
Laulau	A ti leaf package containing pork, salted fish, and taro tops baked in an underground oven or steamed.
Lei	A garland of flowers, fruits, seeds, leaves or ferns.
Limu	Edible seaweed.
Lū'au	Young taro tops baked with coconut cream and chicken or octopus.
Maile	*Alyxias olivaeformis.* A native twining shrub used for decoration and leis.
Makahiki	An ancient festival beginning about the middle of October and lasting about four months, with sports and religious festivities and kapu on war.
Malo	A loin cloth for men made of kapa.
'Ōkolehao	A liquor distilled from the fermented roots of kī.
'Ōlapa	*Cheirodendron.* A native tree with leaves divided into leaflets which move in the slightest breeze.

ABOUT THE AUTHOR
Likeke R. McBride

The author of *The Kāhuna, Versatile Masters of Old Hawai'i* lived in Volcano, Hawai'i for over 30 years until his death in October 1993. A student of Hawaiian tradition and culture, McBride frequently lectured on geology, botany, history and legends of Hawai'i.

Of Irish and Iroquois Indian descent, McBride was born in Reading, Pennsylvania and grew up in Ohio. In 1943 he enlisted in the Navy and after basic training, was assigned to a ship stationed at Nāwiliwili Harbor, Kaua'i. It was there that he fell in love with the Hawaiian Islands and people and started learning the Hawaiian language and about Hawaiian culture.

After service in World War II and the Korean conflict, McBride received a B.S. degree in geology from Ohio State University, with a minor in botany. Following work in industrial research, he joined the National Park Service and was assigned to Hawai'i Volcanoes National Park. With his family, he made his home in the Volcano area. In an eleven year association with Hawai'i Volcanoes National Park, McBride continued to add to his knowledge of all things Hawaiian.

Throughout much of his life McBride was a dedicated student of Hawaiian tradition and culture. He told Hawaiian stories in the old Hawaiian way for nearly thirty years and held a kauila dagger, the sign of a professional Hawaiian storyteller. A talented stoneworker and woodcarver, McBride crafted numerous museum-quality reproductions of Hawaiian tools and weapons.

The author wrote and illustrated four other outstanding original works: *About Hawai'i's Volcanoes; Petroglyphs of Hawai'i; Pele, Volcano Goddess of Hawai'i* (currently out of print); *and Practical Folk Medicine of Hawai'i.*

Books by the PETROGLYPH PRESS

ABOUT HAWAI'I'S VOLCANOES
by L. R. McBride
A CONCISE HISTORY OF THE HAWAIIAN ISLANDS
by Phil K. Barnes
HILO LEGENDS
by Frances Reed
HINA ~ THE GODDESS
by Dietrich Varez
HOW TO USE HAWAIIAN FRUIT
by Agnes Alexander
JOYS OF HAWAIIAN COOKING
by Martin & Judy Beeman
THE KĀHUNA
by L. R. McBride
KONA LEGENDS
by Eliza D. Maguire
LEAVES FROM A GRASS HOUSE
by Don Blanding
PARADISE LOOT
by Don Blanding
PETROGLYPHS OF HAWAI'I
by L. R. McBride
PLANTS OF HAWAI'I
by Fortunato Teho
PRACTICAL FOLK MEDICINE OF HAWAI'I
by L. R. McBride
STARS OVER HAWAI'I
by E. H. Bryan, Jr.; revised by Dr. Richard Crowe
THE STORY OF LAUHALA
by Edna W. Stall
TROPICAL ORGANIC GARDENING, Hawaiian Style
by Richard Stevens

HAWAIIAN ANTIQUITY POSTCARDS
JOHN WEBBER PRINTS

Notes